Hollywood Steps 101

Hollywood Steps 101

◆

My prescriptions for dealing with addiction, depression, OCD, bi-polar disorder and anxiety.

Jonathan Sheinberg

iUniverse, Inc.
New York Lincoln Shanghai

Hollywood Steps 101
My prescriptions for dealing with addiction, depression, OCD, bi-polar disorder and anxiety.

iUniverse books may be ordered through booksellers or by contacting:

iUniverse
2021 Pine Lake Road, Suite 100
Lincoln, NE 68512
www.iuniverse.com
1-800-Authors (1-800-288-4677)

ISBN-13: 978-0-595-35864-9 (pbk)
ISBN-13: 978-0-595-80321-7 (ebk)
ISBN-10: 0-595-35864-0 (pbk)
ISBN-10: 0-595-80321-0 (ebk)

Printed in the United States of America

For Susan, my wife, my Angel and motivation.

For my children, Thea, Nicholas and Harry who always stood by me.

To my Mother, my true friend, and my Father, the model to living life in the honest lane.

Contents

Acknowledgments

This book could not have been written without the support and guidance of my shrink, Dr. Phil Stutz, Father of "X." Dr. Stutz gave me the tools and guidance I needed to heal. He didn't write me off as a "lunatic" or an "imbecile," but as a bright guy who just needed some discipline, structure and consistency in his life.

When you're feeling powerless, out of control, when access is limited to you and your wife, when your kids, your business, and your self-discipline are all going to hell, study the principles in this book to regain the power to go on.

Introduction

Famed Hollywood Executive Tumbles Into Addiction Chaos and Recovers. It is not only a tabloid cover; it is the story of my life.

Faced with constant uncertainty and inner numbness throughout my life, I turned to drugs and gambling. In this book, I will share how I overcame addiction, anxiety, depression and developed coping methods for dealing with obsessive-compulsive disorder (OCD).

Over the years, I found that it had been hard for me to "feel." I had already felt a wild ride with train trips, all-nighters, disco days, an early marriage, a "love child" and a phenomenal career in the entertainment business.

Growing up in Beverly Hills, I got the opportunity to do things that most people only got to dream of doing. My father, Sid Sheinberg, served as President and Chief Operating Officer of MCA/Universal Studios, and I lived the "good life" as a teenager. My beautiful mother, Lorraine Gary who made her debut in *Jaws* was just as into acting as she was politics. Me, I started various businesses, owned many cars, credit cards, and signed various recording deals. There was even a point in time when I lived in Switzerland and got to travel throughout Europe to enjoy the world's most beautiful architecture. I cannot imagine anything will ever top the years of my youthful indulgence.

Throughout my life my dad constantly reminded me that Universal had a no nepotism rule so I knew I could never work there. Perhaps that was why I developed such a street mentality? I wanted to do everything by myself. I wanted to make it on my own and I did not want or need the help of anyone. Still, I walked around with extreme sadness, a negative self-image, and an overwhelming fear that I would never achieve the level of success my father did.

Between my busy Hollywood jobs, marriage and fathering my love child, I found myself and my loved ones suffering. Forget the weight fluctuations and the glum look on my wife's face; I was suffering internally. I turned to the occasional use of drugs and later adopted a gambling hobby. At this point in my life, I was yet to be diagnosed as highly neurotic and I had feelings of inadequacy. I was working my ass off at Columbia Pictures on some huge pictures like *Absence of Malice, Blue Lagoon, Stir Crazy, Stripes, Tootsie, Gandhi* and *The Big Chill,* before I left to go work at Orion Pictures where as head of production, I worked on the films *Robocop, Platoon, Dirty Rotten Scoundrels, Throw Momma from the Train, Hoosiers, Bull Durham,* and *Silence of the Lams.* Unfortunately, the Academy Awards we won were not enough to save my life.

My life fell apart. My marriage deteriorated very quickly and I had my first encounter with "rehab." I entered a one-year outpatient treatment program at St. John's Hospital in Burbank, California. The program saved my life and gave me the strength to get through some very difficult times, including an investigation by the Securities and Exchange Commission (SEC).

That sober time in my life brought back feelings of shame, guilt and inadequacy. Simultaneously, it marked a wonderful time in my life where I had a chance to start over with a new wife and my beautiful young daughter.

"If only you weren't so defective Jon. You are a dyslexic idiot." My inner voice started to eat away at me. I took special education classes and because being an outcast wasn't enough, I was also feeling neglect from my father. The ensuing fury over being discovered as a kid with a learning disability came back, along with the internal label…another Hollywood offspring screwed up.

Faced with the past pains and the desire to live a happier and healthier life, I began the journey to overcoming feelings of inadequacy, insecurity and anxiety. Along the way, I developed the "Hollywood Steps" and learned to live and enjoy each day more fully.

As a teenager, I was always starting businesses—entering into legal contracts, getting credit cards, buying cars, signing recording deals. Reflecting back, I realize what I enjoyed most was the thrill that along came with those transactions.

I had a few different jobs in the "industry" during my three years of high school. Whether I was working for a high-powered entertainment and management firm in Hollywood, or as an agent at a major Hollywood agency, I was learning the business of entertainment my way. After college, I worked my ass off, first in the advertising department at Columbia Pictures—on pictures like Absence of Malice, Blue Lagoon, Stir Crazy, Stripes, Tootsie, Gandhi, and Big Chill—then at Lorimar Television as an executive in the TV movie department—on shows like Dallas, Knott's Landing, and Falcon Crest.

I took a job as an executive at 20th Century Fox and saw what a major studio did firsthand. After my stint at 20th Century Fox, I received the opportunity to join Orion Pictures as head of production, where I worked on films like Robocop, Platoon, Dirty Rotten

Scoundrels, Throw Mamma from the Train, Hoosiers, Bull Durham, Silence of the Lambs, and a slew of others.

I decided to get focused. I realized that I needed to stay engaged in Hollywood. I knew all the players and the game they were playing. I went on to work at Warner Bros. and produce some very successful films.

When my father chose to leave Universal in 1984, there came an unprecedented opportunity for my father Sid, my brother Bill, and myself to start our own production company and make films at our discretion. The new business would be lucrative, but the stress of getting the company started was hell.

I found myself in trouble when all of my old feelings returned yet again. My father, who was always a studio executive, was now a producer. I always saw myself as this successful guy who made it without working for my dad. My brother really looked up to me. Yes, I had made mistakes, but I also was the oldest and I already had a child. I had experienced things in life that he had not just yet.

Our company made some great films, but of course at some cost to my health and well being. I eventually started using again to stop the pain. Unfortunately, this time the drugs and drinking wasn't enough. I added poker and sports betting to the mix.

Eventually, I hit bottom without even feeling it. I did forget how to "feel." Luckily, I just knew from experience that I had reached my low. I knew that if I wanted to be there for my wife, my two new boys, and my daughter, that I had better get some help.

Getting better took quite awhile. I tried using my shrink, Dr. Phil Stutz, who was great, but ultimately I realized that I needed to get a total evaluation so I could know exactly what my problem was.

After breaking a promise I made to myself, my wife, and my shrink, not to mention the uncountable amount of trips to the hospital for dehydration, I went to Sierra Tucson, a rehab center in Arizona. It was here where I learned that in addition to my addiction.

I was also suffering from obsessive-compulsive disorder, bipolar disorder, and depression. There I was again, diagnosed with a potentially disabling condition that would persist throughout my life. I'm trapped once more, this time by repetitive thoughts and by behaviors that are senseless, distressing, and hard to overcome. Now that I'd been diagnosed with OCD, my secret, repetitive thoughts and behaviors would no longer need to be kept secret.

I knew my OCD developed when I was a teenager, but everyone was so concerned with my dyslexia and left-handedness, that they never noticed. I wondered whether I would ever get to feel some relief. With the dyslexia, learning disabilities, drug addiction, gambling, OCD, and bipolar disorder, it was no wonder I didn't feel. I thought," I don't think simply having acupuncture will work this time; it's going to take hard work."

The most difficult thing a dyslexic can do is read, and for years my job had been about reading scripts and sometimes books. Overcoming the problems created by my dyslexia probably led me to become obsessive-compulsive. I always had to check things over and over, and I was always working on fixing my focus problems and remembering to write down numbers without transposing them.

I never gave myself credit for my transformation. *Jon, the drugs are what transformed you.* I am sure the drugs helped the pain in my head and gave me some relief. I was becoming mentally ill and my central nervous system was tweaked.

Maybe my frontal cortex was defective.

Do not let people label you by your flaws. This will shatter your self-esteem and confidence, the way it did mine. Do not let yourself be ridiculed. We are not dumb, we just learn differently. Most of us are above average actually. It's not a disease. My left-handedness also made me feel special.

Everyone in the sixties and seventies wanted to change left-handed people into right-handed people. Kids these days could never fathom something so stupid. I am happy to say that "lefties" are more likely to be musicians, U.S. presidents, MENSA members, and a slew of other prestigious things. I liked being different.

This book is dedicated to helping people recover from alcoholism and other addictions. I explore many aspects of addiction, including its' relationship to the social, economic, and psychological pressures we experience in everyday life. I also explore the role of spirituality, as well as twelve-step programs. I hope this book will help you to find recovery and freedom from whatever is bringing you down.

No touching, kissing, romances. No flirting, no phones, radios, CD players, computers, magazines. No tight fitting clothing, Lycra, bare midriffs. This stay in Sierra Tucson had a profound impact on me. Being in a place where everyone was focused on being healthy and displaying healthy behavior and living was a total shock. No more bong hits or poker runs. No more sports bets or checking the lines on games. No more hiding.

So what was the score on those games I bet on right before I got here? Anyone want to play cards? Can't wait for family week to begin so all that unpredictable shit can come up.

Off I went to my psychiatric evaluation, my physical, and my psychological questionnaire. I better get to know where the activities building is as well as the mental health lecture, the fitness consultation, the 12 step meetings, the psycho and grief meetings and one on ones, spirituality consults and roundtable presentations.

Anyone looking at me from the outside would have thought I had everything. I mean, I had money and I had looks. I had a mom and dad, a nice house and a little brother. I had all of the toys a kid could want, and a complete set of grandparents on both sides. It seemed like no matter what I did with my life, I could never earn back enough to get even.

Chaos

I underwent various assessments and diagnostic tests. Therapists, Family members and Friends who were concerned about my well being had forced me to go to a treatment center and have my total psychological health evaluated. I was worried that I might be suffering from depression, obsessive-compulsive disorder (OCD), bipolar disorder, maybe attention deficit disorder (ADD), or attention deficit/hyperactivity disorder (ADHD).

I was concerned about the possibility that I had developed an eating disorder. Basically, my life was going to hell. This book addresses the causes of compulsion and anxiety. My years of experience tell me that anxiety disorder is a common illness that has complex risk factors related to genetics, brain chemistry, and personality, as well as life events, especially if you're stuck in the line of work I am in. Hollywood can kill you.

Some of us are excessive worriers. We worry about our health, career, money—they're all favorites. Anxieties can make us tremble and can cause us to have trouble falling asleep. In my case, anxiety caused severe abdominal problems.

Some of us get obsessive-compulsive disorder, or OCD, which causes persistent, usually unpleasant thoughts that reflect and exaggerate our fears. People with OCD try to ease their anxieties by engaging in repetitive acts. People with contamination fears, for example, wash their hands and/or repeat phrases.

Maybe now I can stop obsessing about the upcoming family events in my life or about that Christmas or Thanksgiving that made me sick with anxiety for week's prior.

I spent too much time allowing my ex-wife to bully me. Fighting was her drug of choice at the time and I soon discovered that in some ways, bullies find fighting to be a turn-on. Every event seemed like a "symbolic event," and every issue was magnified out of proportion.

Whether you've got new wives or old wives, child support or families to support, dealing with these stresses is a lot harder when you suffer from OCD. You might relive past bad events over and over and over, or suffer from social anxiety and feel like other people are judging or ridiculing you. This can lead to avoidance, phobias, or a life where you have recurring thoughts, impulses, and doubts all day long. You might wonder if you remembered to turn off your coffee maker or if your home and workplace are orderly enough. These thoughts can become repetitive and ritualized, and the relief is only temporary. Before you know it, you would find yourself constantly cleaning, checking, hoarding, even gambling or using drugs and alcohol. These behaviors usually begin in adolescence and gradually work their way into adulthood if they are not stopped.

But, anxiety is treatable. I hope the suggestions offered in this book will help individuals dealing with anxiety. I have suffered through it all. These pages contain a combination of behavior therapy, where you can work on modifying your behavior; cognitive therapy, designed to change the unproductive and harmful patterns that you create; and relaxation techniques.

Anyone experiencing the pain of anxiety, and falling into addictive patterns, needs to first get sober enough to start to "feel" again. You must feel pain as well as the need to be heard and listened to, safely. Sharing is a crucial part of a successful recovery. Whether it happens in a room full of AA people, with a friend, a loved one, or a psychiatrist, it's important to realize that those feelings of anxiety and panic and terror and inadequacy will go away little by little if you follow some of the suggestions listed in this book.

Mental sickness is between your ears. Want to hear God laugh? Tell him your plans. Reality can be hell when you are just visiting.

Although I was born in New York City, I grew up in California. My early family life was intense and stressful. I had extremely high energy as a baby, and I am not sure that I benefited from much parenting or discipline. Both of my parents were very self-willed and self-absorbed; our relationships were strained. During my childhood and teenage years, I had a very close relationship with my brother, my only sibling, but it had since become strained. We drifted apart.

When I was a child, my parents were madly in love with me. They really were. They gave me the best they could, but they were too young, as parents, to really understand how to handle an overactive child.

I was a victim of loving but inadequate parenting.

My father never got below an "A" in his entire life. My grandparents even had a special room in their house that displayed all of the trophies and report cards he received. They were all perfect. I can't believe all I did then at two years old was bang my head against the wall.

I graduated from high school in 1976, a year early, and went to college in Switzerland. A couple years later, I returned to Los Angeles to attend the Immaculate Heart College. I was thinking about becoming a teacher or an oceanographer.

Today I have a belief in a higher power. Even though I was born Jewish, I am not active in the Jewish faith. I believe in the efficiency of twelve-step programs, but I also like to work on my own, within a spiritual framework. I have three children and live with my second wife, who is a wonderful person. While I am always there for my family, I find myself constantly needing to work on family communication issues.

In the past, social situations were very difficult for me, and I had a tendency to withdraw from them. My friendships had been disjointed, and I had relied on my wife, my mother and father, my shrink, my doctors, my gambling psychologists, and a slew of naturalists to act as my support system.

Working had been a way of life for me since I was ten. My first job was throwing newspapers in Beverly Hills. During high school, I worked as a busboy at a Chinese restaurant and as an assistant in a high-powered management company. I soon began my career at Columbia Pictures. From there I moved on to Lorimar Pictures, then to 20th Century Fox, then on to Orion Pictures and President of a major production company at Warner Bros. Studios.

For the past seven years, I have worked full-time with my family, mainly my brother and father. I had this feeling of being stifled or stuck, even though my father is supportive of my branching out and doing other things. I have many years of experience in the entertainment industry, but now I had decided to pursue writing.

A successful career was far from everything. I faced addiction, mood disorders, depression, and anxiety symptoms. Although antidepressants brought me some relief, I still needed those mental strategies to survive.

I went through a party and drug experimentation phase in my high school years. I dealt drugs, surfed, played sports and had a girlfriend. I went from smoking Acapulco Gold and attending Bar Mitzvahs to doing cocaine, LSD, Angel Dust and nitrous oxide. I also had a very passionate relationship with a girl who lived with me from 8th-11th grade. She decided to join me in Switzerland after I had been there for a year.

The few relationships I had were very intense. Some of the women I was with got pregnant, and some of them had abortions. I always had women who loved me just sitting around wondering where I was. I put my parents, my life, and my family on hold while I enjoyed my "lifestyle." I had an urge to mate early in life; a constant search for intimacy and the fear of being abandoned.

All night coke binges, dealing drugs, loveless sex, and unplanned trips to Vegas, or going to San Onofre for surfing was my way of life. My parents were somewhat clueless and just too busy to deal with me.

I have lost an uncountable amount of friends to this disease. Looking back, I cannot believe I'm still alive.

The Eighties

The eighties were a very busy time for me. I had recently returned from Switzerland, and I felt like there were important events going on all around me, especially at Universal Studios. My overly busy dad had maneuvered Universal through a massive period of TV and film production and had expanded the company's music business. His company also added a number of attractions to the studio tour in Los Angeles, including rides based on American assets like Jaws, Back to the Future, E.T., Earthquake, and the Hanna-Barbera characters.

My father's contribution to Universal also included hotels, cable companies, technology, and the Universal CityWalk. My dad's hectic schedule meant he was less available to me than he already was, practically and emotionally.

My dad's hectic schedule meant he was less and less available to me, practically and emotionally. I spent a full year flopping around Beverly Hills, mostly just misbehaving until I found something to focus on. I knew that a prior president of Universal's motion picture division had moved to Columbia Pictures, and I thought maybe he could help me out. I sent him a script with a string and a note taped to it. It read, "I bet once you put this on your finger, you won't be able to stop reading."

I got the call to come in.

It was waiting in the outer office of this important executive, where I had an epiphany. *Screw the script. Ask for a job.* I was in the business. My most valuable attribute was my ability to speak and sell with enthusiasm, so the executive placed me in the motion picture advertising and publicity department.

I worked incredibly hard at Columbia and was promoted to senior publicist. I started a new department: Broadcast Promotions. This department produced electronic press kits (EPKs) for the first time. From that, we would calculate the value of these exposures on TV and cable outlets and generate a report to the top execs at the studio.

As a senior publicist I had the chance to work across the country placing these pieces and attending premieres and press junkets around the country. I also ran Columbia's college campaign, a national program in which company representatives marketed Columbia's films on major college campuses across the country. I was happy, feeling very useful and accomplishing things every day that benefited my employer.

Columbia had hit films such as Tootsie, The Karate Kid, and Ghostbusters. TV hits like The Jefferson's, All in the Family, and Sanford and Son. For the first time in my life, I felt part of something incredible. I worked on movies such as Stir Crazy, Absence of Malice, Gandhi, The Big Chill, Blue Thunder, and Ghostbusters. Being part of a larger team had a profound impact on me and my career. I never had that before. I wasn't riding on my dad's coattail. I became successful on my own. I excelled in a certain area of the entertainment business that was different from my fathers. *Maybe you'll get his attention this time.*

At the same time, I was smoking a joint every day on the way to work, where I was putting in fifteen-hour days. Meeting and celebrating with the likes of Ivan Reitman, Sydney Pollack, Ray Stark, Dustin Hoffman, and Jessica Lange was amazing. When Gandhi won its' multiple Academy Awards, I was there celebrating with Sir Richard Attenborough and Ben Kingsley at the Oscars.

Being a part of The Big Chill was also unforgettable. I could relate to the simple premise of old college friends getting together for a weekend to celebrate the life of a recently deceased friend. The musical score for this film was great, and the trips to NYC to arrange the MTV tie-ins at the beginning were legendary.

I will also never forget working on Ghostbusters. Audiences loved the concept of a group of parapsychologists starting a ghost-hunting service. The film earned $270 million on its initial theatrical release and made Dan Aykroyd and Bill Murray household names.

I should ask my dad how I could earn more money. He said that I needed to get on the creative side.

I was able to get an interview with the president of a relatively new but successful company, Lorimar. This company had been formed in the late '60s by two guys who named it after their ex-wives. It produced successful shows like The Walton's, Dallas, and Full House.

My first job at there was as a director of movies and miniseries. I became familiar with script development, network television, I learned what agents did, and I discovered how to find writers and directors. I also learned how to make a script become more valuable.

Because my boss was hated, people were drawn to me when they needed anything. My work at Lorimar was a great segue into the motion-picture production business. I began working in the movie division at 20th Century Fox, again as director of movies and mir iseries. After Fox repeatedly turned down the films I wanted to make, like Lethal Weapon and Bill & Ted's Excellent Adventure, I left.

I was fortunate that a company called Orion Pictures was looking for a new head of production. I got the job because Mike Medavoy gave me a chance. I was finally going to make six figures, along with stock options. This was the thrill of a lifetime. It was an opportunity that changed my life in many ways and was one of the best professional relationships I ever had.

Learning from the pros was a fantastic experience. Mike Medavoy, Bill Bernstein, Eric Pleskow, and Arthur Krim, were a group of executives who had developed their own philosophy, and their way of working was unparalleled. *GO AWAY party Jon.* The respect they had for talent and filmmakers was like no one else, and I was really proud to be part of their team. Even though my OCD ruled at Orion, I was able to keep on task and my alter ego, Party Jon, was held at bay.

Ultimately, the armor was starting to crack and things were falling apart one piece at a time. Day-to-day work activities like running marketing meetings, tracking producers and agents and managing productions were still functioning, but in my head, things were changing, including my marital status. *You'll be single again soon Jon.* My marriage was deteriorating.

Orion was green-lighting Woody Allen films without even reading the scripts. They believed! Medavoy really welcomed me into the inner circle. He had relationships with people like Jim Cameron, Arnold Schwarzenegger, Warren Beatty, and Barbara Streisand.

He also believed in Jonathan Demme, Kevin Costner, Sean Penn, David Mamet, Oliver Stone, and John Milius, among many others.

It was all too good to be true. We were described as the little engines that could by a cover story in New York Magazine.

Mike taught me how to put films together. I learned how important it was to back the filmmaker and to maintain subtle intervention so they would keep coming back. We won many Oscars using this method, and we were considered the "Tiffany" studio. Our budgets were sparse, and we spent hardly any money on development, but our approach worked.

Among our hits were Hannah and Her Sisters, FX, Back to School, Something Wild, Platoon, Bull Durham, Married to the Mob, Mississippi Burning, Robocop, Dances With Wolves, and Silence of the Lambs. We were on a roll and loving it. I was part of the success. Unfortunately, I was also hitting a new kind of bottom. There I was with an impending divorce, fatherhood, tons of reading and working in a highly competitive environment. That was the start of my collapse. *Haven't proved shit to your father Jon.*

After I had returned from college and decided that I wanted to work full time in Hollywood, I had dabbled with things. I went through times when I didn't do drugs, but there were also times when I relied on marijuana to keep me calm enough to get through the workday. I tended to go back and forth from being clean and sober to being dependent on drugs. Thankfully, even when I wasn't sober, I was always highly functioning, always efficient, and always reliable.

I believe that I inherited certain problems from my parents, like anxiety and depression, not to mention the way I dealt with emotional pain. Even my maternal grandfather showed signs of depression. He had suicidal tendencies, probably overdosed on pills, and at some point in his life, abused food. I myself recently struggled with eating disorders, which would explain the binge eating I did in the 70s.

I was overweight as a teenager, and I took the weight-loss drug Fen-Phen in my early and mid-thirties. I developed a stomach disorder in my forties, and all of these problems were emotionally overwhelming for me. I began using marijuana and buying and selling exotic brands like Cush and Chronic. At the same time, I was in treatment programs to prevent cycles of relapse.

My out-of-control gambling and marijuana use concerned everyone in my family. Especially when my addictions got so bad that AA and GA meetings were not enough. The increased stress I was feeling, combined with the damage caused by the verbal and emotional abuse I experienced in my early childhood, left me with a lot of shame and guilt.

Jonny's Story

When I was very young, I would bang my head against my head-board until I fell asleep. My mom was wondered, "What's wrong with Jonny?" Next thing I knew, I was writing with my left hand and things felt odd.

"We will fix him. Let's give him a drug and he'll get better." My parents always opted for the quick fix. As you might have guessed, that did not work. Then they said, "Let's make him start using his right hand and then he will be better." They tied my left hand behind my back and forced me to use my right hand. *Idiots.* "That will fix Jonny."

Next thing I knew, "Jonny's got dyslexia. Let's put him in a special class. That will fix him."

Can you see where I am going with this? Because of these problems, Jonny became ashamed, and his self-esteem deteriorated. With time, the situation only got worse. This was the beginning of Jonny's depression.

The good thing about Jonny was that he really had feelings. He just had too many at once. Seeing an ill or crippled person, or seeing a film that moved him, would make him tear up inside. As Jonny grew older, the fear and shame grew worse.

Next, social anxiety sank in, along with major anger and resentment. Why hadn't someone talked to him and realized what was wrong? All of Jonny's problems could have been eased. Instead, he was left to take care of himself.

Every now and then, Jonny would figure out a temporary cure for the pain by exercising really hard until the endorphins kicked in.

Childhood overeating and having no knowledge or coping is what led to my drug experimentation, and so the story goes…

Eventually, Jonny stopped being able to see the train coming and he became more self-deluded and disorganized, to the point of not being able to see clearly at all. Unresolved family issues also aggravated Jonny's low self-esteem and contributed to his fear of abandonment. He created a defense mechanism to deal with this, which only brought him more harm and pain. His symptoms became more pronounced, and coping became even harder.

Now, as an adult, Jonny has OCD, he is a bit bipolar, and his anxiety causes somatic symptoms such as vomiting. To be free of this trauma, Jonny did what was the hardest thing for him to do: he abstained from it all, stopped taking drugs, stopped gambling, and started to feel the pain and shame of his early childhood and young adulthood.

To be free of this trauma, Jonny did what was the hardest thing for him to do: he abstained from it all, stopped taking drugs, stopped gambling, and started to feel the pain and shame of his early childhood and young adulthood. Jonny reached for a therapeutic strategy that involved twelve-step programs and experts from all fields. He got on the SSRI psychiatric medication and resumed his exercise program. He also began to express feelings in writing and meeting with shrinks. He reestablished communication with his parents and his brother.

Jonny discovered that he had rare strengths; unbound optimism and the potential to gain self-insight. He did not have ADD or ADHD and he scored off the charts with his ability to care. Jonny will make sure this kids do not suffer the way that he did.

Energy Robbers

Give up?

There can be energy robbing going on in your life; your lack of sleep, low sex drive, chronic pain, stressful workplace, unhappy home, or trouble with tobacco, drugs, or alcohol could be permanently destructive to your well being. All that junk food could be killing you and sending your emotions in all directions. Maybe your "prescription" drugs are suitable.

Noticing how much less productive you have been? Are you showing signs of anorexia or alcoholism? Are you blacking or graying out? Are you restless, confused, or in hopeless despair? Are you swelling all over? Are you cold all the time? Do you avoid emotional situations? Do you not exercise or eat well, or play well or get refreshing sleep? How often do you just snap? How often do you get excited and just want the pain to go away…and I mean fast?

Whether you have a problem with food, drugs, gambling, kids, family, or stress, you must understand the principle that requires you to initially have pain and anxiety.

Try these on for size: certain training triggers and adaptation responses:
"Try to eat six meals a day instead of three; make them little."
"Know that overeating is your enemy."

"Don't allow food to be your medicine; make medicine be your food."

"Drink more water."

I had so many energy robbers in my life that ranged from emotional problems with family members to stress at work. I started smoking pot and gambling at a young age, and as a kid I was very distracted, always sneaking out to explore.

The behavior continued as I became an adult. My restlessness was a problem, so as long as I kept moving, I would not have to face the insanity I created in my life. *Run. Run. Run.*

I had an immense fear of being alone. As a kid I was left alone at home with childhood friends, by parents who did not really care about what was up with me; total mind fuck. My thoughts were sad and my feelings were destroyed. Being left with strangers instead of being in the company of loving parents was hard for me to deal with. I became depressed and began to explore drugs, sex, and traveling.

My parents had no permanent help when I was a child. They could not afford it, although we had a cleaner who would come at variance. My dad stayed with me some nights while my mom was out doing plays. My mother stayed with me during the days. She even hired an eight-year-old who lived across the street to watch me so she could sleep from nine until eleven every morning.

My sadness, restlessness, and fear of abandonment worsened while I was in college. At the time, I did not have any emotional outlets like a therapist or a spouse to talk to. I had constantly been screamed at when I was a kid, and I had never learned to have patience. I can remember my father telling me "he quit." He meant he was giving up on me and that my mother would have to deal with me. That signaled the end of my family photos.

Social Arena

Symptoms
Questioning your social skills
Avoiding social interactions
Anxiety regarding family events
Turning negative
Lacking self-esteem
Feeling abandoned

SOCIAL ARENA

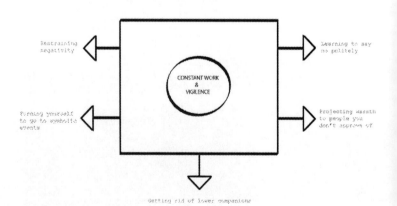

I learned many lessons by examining the social arena we live in everyday. In a perfect world, in the center of the social arena, there would be a display of constant work and vigilance. Outside of that perfect world, we need to learn how to say no politely, and projecting warmth towards people we do not approve of is also important. Force yourself to attend significant events, like open houses at school, dinners with friends, and parties, especially if you do not want to go. Lastly, restrain yourself from negativity and eliminate all lower companions from your life.

Back in the World

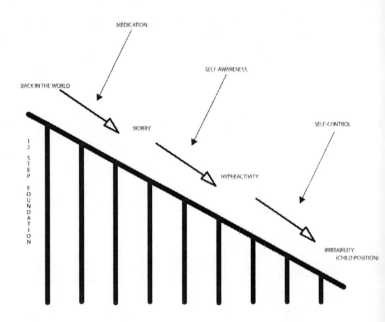

Once you feel you are back in the world, you must balance out your priorities, self-awareness, and self-control, along with medically supervised medication if you need it. Even a twelve-step foundation might help you avoid worry, hyperactivity, and irritability, all of which could cause damage. A weak structure will create more stress for you, as opposed to a disciplined structure, which could cause you and the world to work well; a commitment to the world.

At the center of impulsivity is danger. We tend to start to express emotions too fast, usually in our speech and how we express ourselves. We also try to overcome anxiety too quickly. You must remember to slow down in every way in order to succeed. Either you transform into a super-enchanted state where all the good, creative thoughts back into your heart, or you start to feel dissatisfied and alienated.

This is when impulsivity bombards your entire being. You need to become supercharged. Picture impulsivity in the middle, and imagine yourself fighting it off. You are trying not to allow anxiety to overcome you, while you are also trying not to solve any problems too quickly. Your speech is not going to go faster and faster, and you are not going to express your emotions. You must slow down before it really is too late.

Two-Track Model

Symptoms
Discovered
Without structure

TWO TRACK MODEL
Reward
CREATIVE PATH (EXCITING)
Spiritual Work Supports Creativity WWWWWWWWWWWWWWWWWWWWWWWWWWWWWW High Frequency Meetings!!!
SPIRITUAL PATH (TEDIOUS)
FOUNDATION

I believe in a two-track model. There is the creative path, which is exciting and has rewards, as well as the spiritual path, which can feel tedious yet lets you build solid foundations. Spiritual work could also lead to great creative outcomes.

The moments of your life must be broken down. Imagine a box; at the very bottom is your foundation. You continue to build your spiritual path on top of your foundation. Resting above your spiritual path is a high frequency of meetings. This is where you do a lot of spiritual work, and allow your creativity to show simultaneously. On top of that, you start to build a creative path and a reward. The key of the two-track model is to transform your negative energy.

If the negative energy is not transformed, symbolic events become magnified and the world sees your hate. Your creativity will be misused and wasted. *Relax Jon; it's just an event.*

We can fight off negativity and fear without having to isolate ourselves.

Symptoms
Feeling negative energy
Being a social rebel
Acting or being hateful towards others
Carelessness
At risk

Momentum Must Be Broken

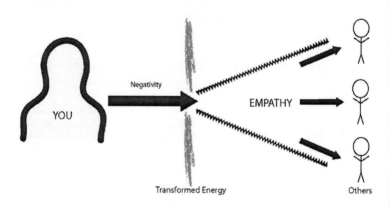

Imagine yourself standing with negativity bouncing off you. Picture yourself transforming all of that energy into empathy for others. Somewhere during the transformation of the energy, the momentum must be broken.

The social world is easy to control if you have the will to heal. Events, meetings, managerial responsibilities, and financial responsibilities are all part of it. Do not let the bad stuff own you. You are not a social rebel. Social rebels allow "X" to attack them and bring them down. They fall into negativity and fear. Before they know it, they are retreating into isolation. "X" is the bad guy. His goal is to pull you off-track; beat you down and destroy you.

Out of the box thinking is my nature. I have to be constantly disciplined if I am to retain creative power. Impulsive behavior only creates hypercritical negativity. Thinking outside of the box is very important.

Symptoms
Lacking discipline
Being critical of others
Impulsive

Creative Power

Consistent Discipline

Outside The Box Thinking

Impulse

Your Nature

Hypercritical
Negativity

Symptoms
Allowing social events to magnify into high pressure
Feeling terror or panic about everyday occurrences
Discouraged
Business problems

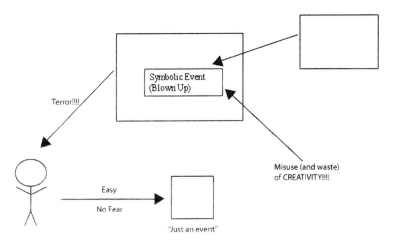

Symptoms
Being in fear
Isolating
Rebelling against the world

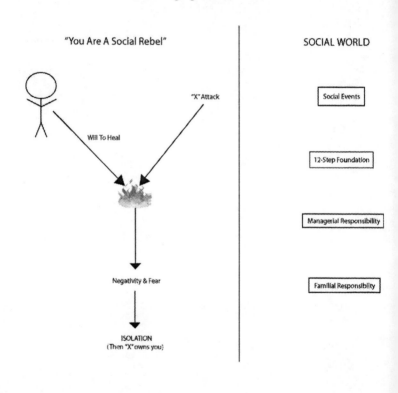

"You Are A Social Rebel"

"X" Attack

Will To Heal

Negativity & Fear

ISOLATION
(Then "X" owns you)

SOCIAL WORLD

Social Events

12-Step Foundation

Managerial Responsibility

Familial Responsiblity

Divine Warnings

Symptoms
Lacking a higher power or God
Lost track of your life's path

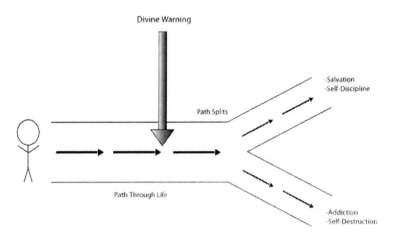

Allowing triggers to send you downward instead of up our lives are full of hidden causes, or triggers, of compulsion. My life had many of them; poker, drug use, isolation. Anything can trigger our addictive or compulsive behaviors, leaving us wondering, once more, "How did I get here again?"

When we start a twelve-step program, we show that we want to stop our destructive behaviors, take stock of ourselves, and start thinking clearly. As we accomplish these goals, problem solving will become much easier and family relationships will improve.

We will be able to devote attention to everyday responsibilities such as budgeting and bill paying. Decisiveness will return, and we will get our personal and professional lives back on track. Our irritating behaviors will start to disappear, and we will feel more relaxed. We will have more time to spend with our families, and we may even gain some insight into ourselves and give affection to others.

Creative salvation happens when you are subjected to a force much stronger than your ego. Perhaps when a God-like power steps into the picture with a divine warning and enables you to practice self-discipline instead of self-destruction. You will find yourself on a "path through life" that splits in at least two different directions.

The road that goes up to the left leads to self-discipline and salvation. The road that goes down to the right leads to self-destruction. As you travel along the path through life, you will receive divine warning before you decide which road to take.

Inner Deadness and Uncertainty

Symptoms
Bored and unhappy
Stressed
Taking destructive risks to relieve anxiety

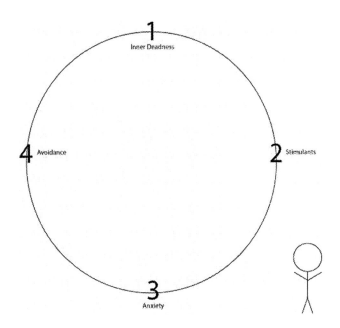

Inner deadness is a circle. Inside that circle are inner deadness, stimulants, anxiety, and avoidance. Picture yourself standing outside that circle, waving your hands with a big smile.

Creating an area that is free of gambling and drugs and that involves daily exercise, a twelve-step program, and a correct diet will purify you. Physical activity is one of the most useful tools in fighting depression. Start with a flexible and pleasurable exercise program. You should exercise four to five times a week, and reap the psychological and physiological benefits. Make your exercise goals realistic so that success will be certain. *Watch out Jon. Here comes the seratonin and dopamine.*

Help in making your short- and long-term problems go away is coming.

Some of your friends and family members are bad influences on you. Unfortunately, sometimes the bad influences in our lives are invested in keeping us "ill." For example, when I was gambling, friend "X" was able to get me pot and keep me out of my families hair.

To be healthy, we need to be in a self-contained structure, free of the bad influences, as the diagram shows. One way to build a good self-contained structure is through love. This takes time, and is diametrically opposed to the immediate excitation you may be seeking.

Symptoms
Being around bad influences
Weakness and impulsiveness
Seeing lower companions that don't belong in your life

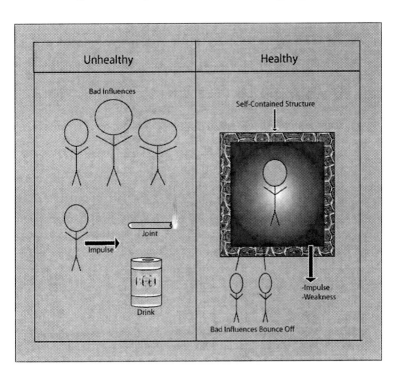

X Marks the Spot

Symptoms
Slipping
Temptations creeping in
Moving too fast
Trying to leave space too quickly

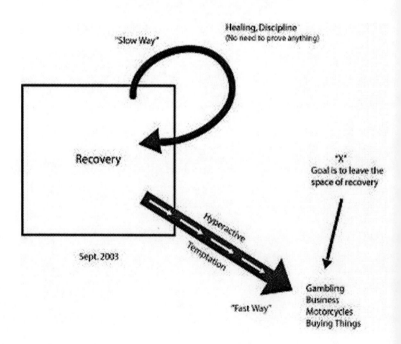

"Slow Way"

Healing, Discipline
(No need to prove anything)

Recovery

"X"
Goal is to leave the
space of recovery

Hyperactive
Temptation

Sept. 2003

"Fast Way"

Gambling
Business
Motorcycles
Buying Things

Picture a box; inside that box is recovery. In order to get inside this box, you can take the slow healing route or you can take the fast destructive route. "I can cure myself." *Dangerous thought Jon.*

While someone is traveling down the fast destructive route, they don't see "X" creeping in the back door and rejoicing in their decision.

The key to recovery is realizing that you can't do it yourself. Acknowledging your defiance and reaching out to the sources of support provided, is crucial. Support might be a family member, a friend, or even a person in a twelve-step program. Whoever it is, keep them around.

Sponsors can also be very helpful in overcoming defiance. The notion of submitting to someone else's direction is very helpful in recovery. The simple exercise of doing the steps and sharing them with another person can be a magical experience that is great for your health. Sharing will relieve your feelings of anxiety, stress, resentment, and shame that you build up daily. This requires submission.

Stop saying "no" before you hear the whole question idiot. Fast answers like this only create more difficulty in your life. *Today is going to suck. Just submit and let the day happen. Submit Jon.* It works.

There are a few ways to approach addiction and treatment. There is the moral way, which uses spiritual deficit and conscious choice. There is also a temperance treatment, which addresses casual factors and advocates treatment centered on abstinence and prohibition. This approach uses specialists who believe that moderation is primary to treatment and that abstinence as an alternative. According to this approach, the drug holds the power. I don't buy it.

We also have the disease model, which suggests that this is an irreversible, and progressive disease caused by abnormal traits inherent in the individual. The individual has a constitutional disease or disorder that can only be treated through identification and confrontation of the condition, lifelong abstinence, and a recovery that involves other individuals, peer support groups, and therapists. I like this model a lot.

The psychological approach to addiction views the various dependencies as rooted in abnormalities of personality and character. This includes poor impulse control, low self-esteem, and the inability to cope with stress, as well as egocentric manipulation traits where there is a need for power. Psychotherapy and behavior modification to improve these deficits is needed.

According to the social education theory, which borrows from classical conditioning, addiction is learned cognitively. It proposes that the person's influences are using reinforcement of good behavior through conditioning and it reduces stressors.

Using environmental interactions and socialization will also result in success. A lot of this can be resolved through realistic goal setting; appropriate modeling, skill training, impulse control and simply knowing about "X."

Withdrawal is difficult. Whether you are addicted to heroin, cocaine, marijuana, methamphetamine, ecstasy, alcohol, painkillers, sex, or gambling, you are dealing with something dangerous that will affect your central nervous system. You are fooling around with the dopamine in your body to get pleasure. This euphoria will lead to hyper-stimulation, reduced mental clarity, irritability, anxiety, and paranoia. Go back to your recovery box. Take the "slow way." This is the only way to go. You will start to love yourself again.

How to Fight Anxiety

Symptoms
Feeling tired or unmotivated
Wanting to feel joy but can't
Isolating/escaping
Starting to act out with compulsive behaviors like gambling, drugs,
alcohol and sex
Pattern of restlessness

HOW TO FIGHT ANXIETY

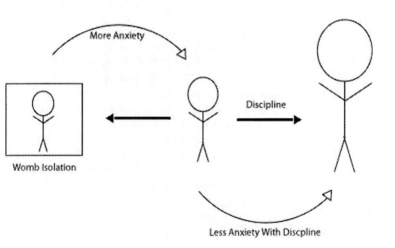

When suffering from anxiety, you may feel like you are in a womb; you have isolating thoughts and you feel trapped, until more anxiety rolls in. You must realize that fighting anxiety leads to healing and success. You can either be prepared for it and fight it by being disciplined and consistent, or you can close your eyes and enter into the womb; isolating yourself. *Don't go Jon. You know where that's going to take you.*

Anxiety will not go away on its' own. Arguments, distrust, unhappiness, and denial are huge causes of it. If you make threats, lose interest, or create imaginary illnesses, anxiety arrives. Losing self-respect creates anxiety. Removing yourself socially, admitting defeat, and living in total fear causes anxiety. Being intolerant, suspicious, irritable, or acting extravagantly or dishonestly will cause anxiety. Irrational behavior, jealousy, and blaming others create anxiety. Some of my past illnesses were surrounding my weight fluctuation and nausea.

Unresolved issues from your past can cause you to feel shame. That screaming parent, special class you had to take, or anything that gave you that feeling of being "less," must be addressed. If not, your other symptoms will become much more pronounced.

Pressures

Symptoms
Feeling a lapse throughout the day
Escaping during that lapse by leaving to gamble, drink, smoke, do
drugs and have sex
Not sure about the pressure you're feeling
Triggers go off in environment

PRESSURES

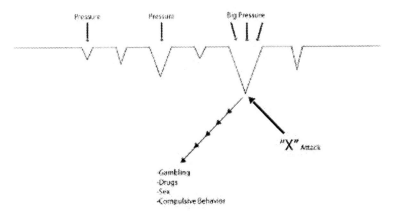

Picture your path through life as a straight line. The little dips you encounter along the way will represent *pressures*. You can withstand these dips if your life is structured. If not, you may fall into the hole of gambling, drugs, sex, compulsive activity, or anything that your "X" may put in front of you. You cannot allow these dips in the road to get bigger. If you fall into the dips they just keep getting bigger and bigger. *Jon you better find something to do.* Consider using meditation and clearing your past as a form of self-healing. Use dreams, visions, and premonitions to learn and grow.

Look in the mirror and imagine that a huge, ugly shadow is staring back at you, totally encompassing your being. Now, imagine a healthy mind and a body that starts to consume food and other things to the point where you have "grossed out thoughts, (gastric illness)" allowing you to stumble upon eating disorders. *Stop it Jon.* Intervene. Make the shadow disappear.

Practicing honesty, trust, and openness is necessary for recovery to take place. It is okay to share your dark secrets with the people you love, as long as you do not hurt anyone. Examine your spiritual self. Finding new friends and being of service will help you to heal. Make amends with anyone you have had conflicts with; resolving interpersonal conflicts can leave you feeling loving and courageous. This is how you create enlightenment and reach higher levels of consciousness.

Because I was willing to change, I could relax, which left me with great optimism. All of my sudden fears went away, and my self-esteem returned. My guilt was gone, and I began to eat, rest, and sleep much better. I regained the respect of my family and friends.

Turning Grandiosity into Peace

Symptoms
Lacking control in work place
Not feeling safe or secure
Not showing managerial control or discipline
Lacking money management skills

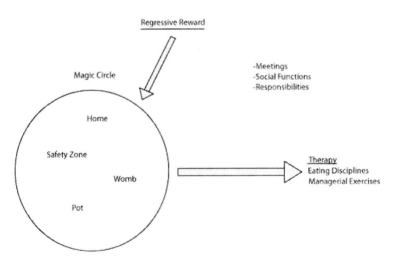

You need a safety zone to help you prepare for stressful events, social functions, or taking care of other responsibilities you may have. This safety zone can be created by giving yourself a regressive reward. The regressive reward setup is necessary if you find yourself being bogged down by daily pressures. I found myself putting off important phone calls that needed to be made.

Regressive awards will allow you to create a safety zone that will not only let you maintain managerial and dietary discipline, but will also give you more control over your life.

Let life exist. Do not let fear drive your behaviors or motivate you to do something you aren't up for. You are entitled to your feelings and to make mistakes and cry. If conversations make you feel diminished or humiliated, terminate them. Strive to be healthier than those around you. Work on being relaxed and on just having fun and playing, and do not forget to set limits for yourself.

When I was younger I suffered from severe behavioral outbursts. I had countless conflicts with my father and my brother. My childhood patterns of paranoia were destroying my life. *Relax Jon.* No matter how many times I told myself to relax, it never worked. *Relax Jon.*

Symptoms
Feeling weak
Acting like a big shot on surface
Irritable
Hyperactive behavior
Making unreasonable plans to cover up losses

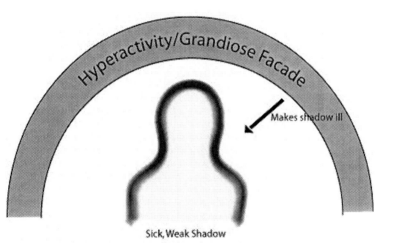

Ever given thought to how your shadow can make you ill?

Let's face it, hyperactivity and a grandiose facade outwardly will ultimately make a sick, weak shadow.

Hyperactivity and grandiosity will ultimately make you feel ill. They will create a weird, huge gray shadow and you will end up sick and weak. Your shadow will bring you down.

If you always think you are winning and you constantly fantasize about being a big shot, you have an ego problem. You are probably unreasonably optimistic, even boastful of your gambling deals and life with drugs and alcohol as well. The false ego acts as a cover for low self-esteem. Eventually you will lose and start to cover everything up. *Jon that's what you did.*

Your work will be affected, and your personality will change. People who are around you frequently will realize that you changed, but you won't. You may become irritable, restless, and more withdrawn. Your bad behavior will just become worse, until you end up lost in panic and remorse, spiritually broke.

Grandiosity will leave you unable to deal with your responsibilities, especially financial ones. Your home life will become increasingly unhappy, and sooner or later, you will find yourself alienated from friends and family. Your reputation, damaged.

Many people get grandiose over money while they are managing products and projects. They typically have visions of huge profits, but their bragging turns into nothing. Other people may laugh at their big plans and make them feel hurt and misunderstood. You really get to see this present itself in Hollywood. People who misuse their position because they either represent important talent or work for a network or studio.

Staying in the Present

Symptoms
Hyperactivity
Not at peace
Anger building
Not trusting
Values slipping
Feeling disconnected
Looking to escape

STAYING IN THE PRESENT

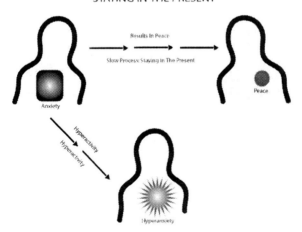

ANXIETY + HYPERACTIVITY = HYPER ANXIETY

Use your life as motivation. Empower yourself to change your life. Today, displaying the familial and managerial consistency that I am able to makes me feel great. *You are head of this house.*

I could not stand to think about the tall African lady my mother hired who constantly clicked her tongue, not communicating with me; or the fat woman who sat on me until my mother came home; or the completely stoned lady from downtown LA who basically drank our cough medicine all day long while my mom was away. All of these memories brought up terrifying feelings of isolation and loneliness. *Eh, you weren't worth fighting for.*

Both anxiety and peace are stored within our bodies. We can ultimately take the proper route to correct our anxiety as long as we slow the process down, stay involved with the process, and work hard towards our end result; peace. You must stay in the present. To do this, find a thought that works in your life and lock into it closely. *There's someone upstairs that's always looking out for me.*

So many things in life are related to self-empowerment and willpower: paying back money you owe, for instance, or realizing that you can solve your problems by sharing them with people. Believing in a higher power can be useful.

When I was a child, simply going through everyday life caused me anxiety. Playing sports helped, but my mind was moving faster than anything else, and I had no one to teach me how to settle down. There was no one I could count on to understand what I was feeling. *Jon why aren't you good enough. What the hell is wrong with you? You obviously need to change.*

Just now, decades later, I am finally figuring things out. Now I know that gambling and all the other stuff screwed me up big time. The addictions I had as a child, then as a teen and later as an adult, were all bad. Creating all of these habits, which I thought were little, were in fact really huge.

Simply asking my brain to stop focusing on bad stuff was important. Hyperactivity, not staying in the present, was also a very difficult part of my life. No matter what I did to escape, the pressure of shame would arise, and the next thing I knew, I would be in the shithouse, not feeling loved, cared for or emotionally safe. I would run to be overly hyperactive.

Inspirational Power

Symptoms
Lacking structure in work and life
Lacking inspiration
Not getting respect from loved ones
Seeing no future
Total uncertainty of outcomes in business dealings or life

Power Positions

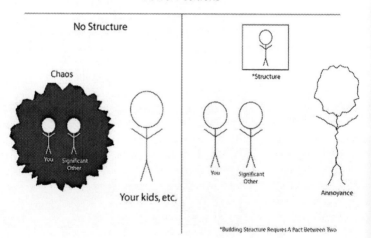

External influences in today's world make it very important that you ask for help if needed and continue to work on control and the power you possess. One way you can gain this power is through inspiration. It is necessary for you to establish a structured connection with your inspirational power. This can be a pact achieved through discipline, with such behaviors as medication, and eating/gambling under control. In asking for this external positive influence, the magic will present itself.

There is something called synchronicity attraction. This means that we attract what we think we want. If you think you want to do drugs, you are going to attract those people who use them. Feeling a desire to better yourself and start exercising will attract healthier people to you. This is where higher and lower companions come into play. It is time to let go of your lower companions and start to attract higher companions with more structure and discipline in their lives.

There are two power positions. For our sake, let's imagine them in a box; on the left side is no structure and on the right side there is structure. Without structure, you and your significant other are in total chaos, with a black cloud hovering over you. Your kids and everybody else are outside of the cloud. With structure, you are contained in a much smaller box. You, your significant other, and everyone else are building a structure that requires an understanding between two. All the annoyances stay outside of the structure.

We all face uncertainty in life. Whether it is in a card game or a possible reaction to a certain drug, dealing with uncertainty takes energy. The only way to recreate this energy is to maintain self discipline and strive for unstoppable will. Focusing your energies towards greatness requires focused energies and an entire unification, with limitations as to avoid resenting life and its pleasures.

The biggest obstacle that stood in my way, was trying to get over the uncertainty of any particular outcome. I couldn't do it. Gambling, smoking and shopping were just some of the behavioral patterns I turned to for that comfortable feeling of certainty; instant certainty. *I hope those guys at Fox liked my script. My job is on the line.*

Symptoms
Feeling resentful
Feeling limited
Powerlessness

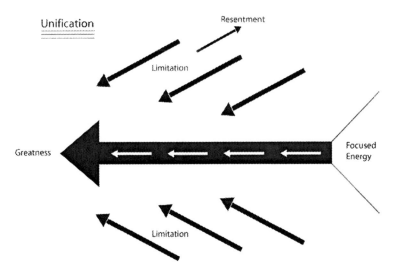

Channel of discipline

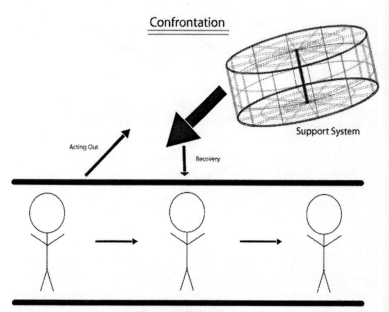

Confrontation

Support System

Acting Out

Recovery

Channel Of Discipline

Imagine a straight line, with focused energy flowing through its center. This energy leads to greatness. Above and below this straight line are limitations. However, also above the line, are all kinds of resentments. You must focus your energy to go through the middle of the line, towards greatness. This is the Channel of discipline.

Staying in this channel will keep you safe and in control, or in recovery mode. If you travel outside of the channel, you may face confrontations. Stay in recovery. Create support systems. Stay in that focused energy channel in the center, and you will achieve greatness. Limitation and resentment are old news.

Strive to build a strong career, family, and foundation in the channel of success, and brighten up the world with your higher state of mind. Provide wonderful leadership, and you will earn respect and love from those you serve well. Remember, if you succumb to drugs, bad diet, inconsistency, gambling, or any other destructive behaviors, the only way back is to maintain respect for yourself and to maintain consistent leadership, with your mind in a higher state.

Structure is so important. You must keep this in mind in order to keep "X" out of your life. Practicing a twelve-step program and using self-restraint will help you recover from anything self-destructive. I also found that getting into the core structure, or the center of you, is the key. If that process is ignored, or you try to do without the structure, you may start acting out: spending money, gambling, using drugs, drinking, becoming verbally or physically abusive. Depression and withdrawal may also rear their ugly heads once again.

Impulsivity

Symptoms
Allowing anxiety to control your behavior
Giving into pressure by showing fast speech or careless decisions
Lacking routine in life

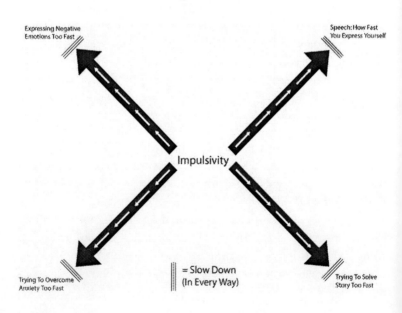

If impulsivity is at the center of your life, you might express yourself and your emotions too fast or try to solve your problems too quickly. You must learn to slow down. Try to stay centered. Be optimistic and tolerate the uncertainty of transition.

You must possess and process more. You never know when your insight will come. When this does happen, it will be a profound experience. Do not force the miracle. Everything in life is a miracle composed of beauty, tension, and drama: one third will be great; one third will be bad; and one third will get the job done. If we gain insight from experience, we are growing. Be willing to do things you do not think you can do. Stretch yourself and go outside into the world and breathe, especially if you don't feel like it.

Change what you think needs changing. When I don't feel like doing something it means that I need to do it. I know that it's healthy for me to go through with activities, such as dates or dinner parties that I would rather avoid. Practice letting it all go. Ride loose in the saddle of life. Forget about fairness because Life is equally fair to all. Be humble and grateful.

Try to write down your thoughts every day before acting on them. Be persistent in all the things you need to do. Remember the story of the tortoise and the hare. Pray, meditate, whatever. Keep your perspective, and try not to sweat all the small stuff. Breathe, in and out…and I mean breathe. And do not smoke cigarettes. Remember to put first things first, no matter what. Since you are taking it all one day at a time, try not to cut corners. Know thyself, and tolerate all the things that are thrown your way. Try to practice self-reflection in your life, so you can see it more clearly.

Remember that whatever your disease, compulsive gambling, alcoholism, or eating disorders, they are all progressive. If you are psychologically out of control and preoccupied with your destructive urges, then they are there. If you are driven to any of these the way an addict needs drugs, you are it. Soon you will need it as a mood elevator, just so you can exist. It will become more and more difficult to resist, and it will eventually affect all aspects of your life. You must learn to come to grips with this issue of destruction and understand that you cannot control or manage it. Accept this. Address it. If not, just know that two out of every three of my teenaged friends are dead. That's right, no longer living. *You are luckier than you know.*

Think about who was involved in your addiction and where you usually practiced your addiction. When did your addiction begin? And what exactly happened? *The Days of Denial I called them.*

You might have thought you could cut it down anytime: less gambling, less drinking, and less drugs or sex. Or that you would only do it certain times of the day, or you would switch from harder things to softer things. *Instead of shooting up, I'll just smoke a jay.*

Can you describe the first time you used anything? Was it drugs, alcohol, or gambling? Did you enjoy these phases? What was your emotional state during these experiences?

Describe the prolonged losses you've suffered from these defects. Describe how you and others have tried to cover them up. How much time did you spend on these issues? Did you manipulate things to keep it going? Did you experience anything devastating?

You soon realize what you have; friend problems, legal problems, family problems, isolation, low self-esteem, anxiety, thoughts of depression, lies, cheating, and some other fabulous things.

Your sleeping and eating patterns are also affected. In general, physical deterioration occurs, leaving us with greater damage in areas of our family, with fights occurring and issues with everyone from spouses to kids to siblings. This can create extreme guilt and low self-esteem. In my case, it caused many trips to the doctor and sometimes even the emergency room. I also worried the hell out of my loved ones.

Do you have to guess what normal life is like? Do you have a hard time following things through to completion? Do you lie? Are you without mercy for yourself? Do you have a hard time having fun? Do you take yourself too seriously? Are intimate relationships hard for you? Do you worry about abandonment, or about being criticized and judged? Do you manage your time poorly so that it works only for you? Try to write a paragraph describing any of these situations in your life.

Addictions and related problems are mainly caused by some inner craving to discover one's true self. Recovery solutions include taking responsibility for everything: for what we eat, for substances we ingest, and for our relationships. We can find balance and true satisfaction in good living, which can keep self-destructive behavior at bay.

A breakdown in our ego structure causes us to turn to bad habits to feel better. When quitting anything, people feel oppressed by their own unrelenting ego structure. Abstinence causes irritability, nervousness, and insomnia, but you can do it. Look at America. In this country, there are ten million alcoholics, two hundred thousand heroin addicts, seventy million overweight people, and a hundred million caffeine addicts. *That's you! You're a caffeine addict aren't you?* Do you know any caffeine addicts?

Our professional lives need to have new meaning, and bring us happiness and fulfillment. Work needs to give us a sense of freedom, dignity and self-reliance. Alienation from yourself will create alienation from creative labor. You cannot lose touch with basic human experiences.

Addictions are spiritual emergencies. We turn to addictions to temporarily ease our emotional pain and suffering. Materialism can also cause this. Measuring yourself by your social position and material wealth is wrong. When we do this, emptiness and unhappiness may set in, as may alienation from self and an unbalanced focus on professional success or sexual pleasure.

Humans are skillful at hiding and repressing their feelings of unworthiness. I believe we begin picking this skill up at birth. Look at society today. People know more about using their cell phones and TV sets than they do about caring for kids (except for my beautiful wife Susan). Doesn't that make every child feel less worthy? We all need validation, especially from our parents, but our parents are too busy seeking professional and material success.

As kids, and then as adults, we start to bottle up our feelings. We become great at covering up our hurt. Whether it comes from gambling losses, drug use, or accidents in life, the body retains pain, suffering, and denial.

Most of us looking for answers to addiction or other issues have moderate to high levels of depression and anxiety. For me, stomach discomfort occurs. For years I thought I had a medical problem, and I had all types of medical evaluations. Now, I understand that I convert my emotional distress into gastrointestinal distress. We need to work on health, self-esteem, goals, values, work, play, and relationships every day.

How much of your time on earth have you spent well? Do you find yourself expressing yourself with pressured speech or walking funny? Did you know that your ability to articulate is greatly affected by your mood? My thoughts tend to get more organized but extremely critical when I am focusing on other people rather than my own feelings. All the feelings have had to be constantly focused along with my inside judgment and cognition.

Some people have adult ADD. If you have concentration issues, or focus and memory issues, it is possible that you have it. Sometimes this problem coexists with anxiety and depression, and may eventually improve over time. Others, including me, have been diagnosed with OCD; we may suffer from contamination and germ fears and engage in behaviors such as hoarding, saving, cleaning, and counting. OCD will interfere with your daily life unless you work on it.

I have some long-term personality issues to work through. I am depressed, pessimistic, and overly energetic. I have a somber approach towards life, and severe anxiety in social situations. I find it hard to express my anger in a straightforward way by being honest and assertive. Instead, I repress my anger and then act out passive aggressively with sarcasm.

I often look towards others for emotional guidance and support. I often act wounded so that I can elicit sympathy from people. I have feelings of low self-esteem, self-worth, and self-doubt. *That's why I have addictive behaviors.* Today, I get to practice these principles and exude and outflow of love and empathy for others.

I seek the quick fix to difficult and complex life problems and situations. For example, if I was in a situation that was making me upset, and the situation got worse, I would act even more impatient and impulsive and engage in even more unpredictable behavior.

Transformation

It is important to see yourself through your own eyes and not through the eyes of others. If you are honest and feel strongly about things to the point of getting angry, try to work your feelings out internally as well as externally; this may even be that you feel hurt or confused and need to talk things out with someone you trust.

Taking physical and mental health for granted is wrong. Disorders like diabetes, high blood pressure, heart disease, and depression all occur when you do not exercise. We tend to ignore problems like stress and depression. Physical activity has psychological benefits, especially with stress-related illness, worrying, and self-doubt. Worriers benefit from exercise the most. Stress can manifest itself in symptoms ranging from muscle tension to stomachaches. Exercise can also make you less angry and irritable and reduce hypertension.

You will sleep better and wake up feeling more invigorated when you exercise regularly. Choose a variety of physical activities so that your exercise regimen does not get boring. Never tell yourself that you are too stressed to exercise. Working out will only reduce your stress and help you think more creatively. Consider yoga, walking, running, cycling, light weightlifting, or swimming. Try anything to change the cycle.

We have admitted that we were powerless over alcohol, drugs, and gambling, and that our lives have become unmanageable. We were defeated and we admit it. We went to AA bankrupt and gained something back. Humiliation gave way little by little.

My admission of powerlessness set the course for the miracle to begin. I was no longer fighting with the monsters in my head, or hearing those tapes replay the bullshit over and over. The obsession is in my mind; it is mental, as everyone in recovery would know. There is no way I can control the addictions and obsessions at all. Daily repetition proves this.

Most people wait until they hit bottom to give up their addictive behaviors. I would buy just enough pot to last until I quit, and gamble until the next week, telling myself I would quit then. I wouldn't throw away pipes, papers, old pot pills or even casino chips. But I know I should have flushed it all down.

I believe that a power greater than ourselves can restore us to sanity. Believing in a power greater than ourselves should be simple, but we need to work on this daily. Have you been through the first steps so that by now you are clean and sober? This is the most important thing. What is stopping you? Are you waiting to hit bottom?

You could use the large group that AA had at your meetings to be your higher power until you are able to relax and gain some spiritual insight. Only minimum faith is needed. The rest will come.

It is easy to forget the importance of a higher power when you run out on your disease. Strive for quality faith, and do not keep making unfulfilled pledges to fix your problems. *Pray Jon.* Keep your mind open, whatever your faith is. All you need is to have some faith and some willingness to start the process. Just try to crack the door open a bit, and the light will come.

This requires action. Turn your stuff over, and step out of that old self will that keeps you disconnected from a higher power or God. It seems like a bitch, but try it, and do not be stubborn.

Memories have emotional power, and we are often highly selective about which ones we choose to call up. Some memories have a negative impact. Remembering a negative event can bring back the emotions connected to it; the memory triggers our brain to release neuro-chemicals.

We should practice thinking about enjoyable memories, so that our brains release positive chemicals instead. *Oh Jon, you have hot air ballooning memories with your wife, coaching soccer games for Nicholas and Harry and the birth of Thea.* There is solid research that shows memories of addictive behaviors cause the release of dopamine to please a euphoric recall, which can override the so-called executive functioning of the prefrontal cortex, the area of the brain responsible for decision-making. Death, power struggles, and mood changes will only cause us to have these self-full-filling thoughts of negativity.

All of your memories are stored in your brain. They affect feelings, thoughts, and movement. Obsessiveness and worrying are issues for me all of the time when I'm with my family, for example, or when I am learning something new at work.

Feeling negative about the future can also have an affect on us. Knowing you always have options is very important. Worrying and holding onto your past can hurt and so can getting stuck on certain thoughts and behaviors, causing you to act out negatively. If you are constantly thinking about that one time you got high and how good you felt, the chances of you getting high again are pretty likely. Get those thoughts out of your head. *I remember the time my daughter Thea was born.*

As your self-esteem increases, you can hear critical comments from people and actually appreciate their honest feedback, rather than respond in an aggressive or defensive manner. You may actually start to welcome people's comments and insights into behaviors you might not see as negative. Being argumentative or uncooperative automatically causes negative things to happen. For example, let's say I was dwelling on something that hurt me in the past, and some-one offered me a truthful reflection about what I needed to change. Because I was dwelling in negativity and hurt, I would react defen-sively and reject the needed feedback. Addictive behavior, along with eating disorders and road rage, result from holding onto nega-tive emotions; we injure ourselves instead of hurting the person we are mad at.

I started gambling as a young kid. I was barely seventeen, but old enough to drive to Vegas with a friend who was also seventeen. *Ha, we looked about 21.* We always had a good time and usually walked away with winnings after the first day. Gambling went from being fun to being an addiction that ruined all aspects of my life. This pathological gambling started with a big win. I could not shake the memory of the high I got from winning. *Damn that felt good.* I was compelled to chase those feelings until they self-destructed. I was brainwashed by the casino industry. I associated Vegas and gam-bling with pleasure, even when I did not win.

Singing in the shower, or just showering, can be helpful for your brain. Singing and doing yoga are joys of life, almost spiritual expe-riences. These experiences resonate throughout the body. This is even true with little kids in preschool. The kids are taught to stop playing and work. Natural play is squashed by the societal need to "grow up."

All destructive behaviors disturb patterns in the brain. An overall toxic thing happens, where less physical activity turns into less opportunity for neurological rewards.

Eventually, the world becomes constricted and limited, so that satisfying the addiction becomes the only pleasurable thing. This leads to a deficit in play and pleasure, and society teaches us to play its' way. At some point, the emotional appeal of all the psychological issues must wear out.

I could only live with the family issues and real life issues for so long. My brain had been altered over time, but knew it was time to stop obsessing. Now I can be free of the cravings and desires as long as I am passionate and energized about my life, and not my addictive behaviors.

Winning Level

Symptoms
Childhood scripts in head dominate our thinking
Judging others with immediate bad thoughts
Compulsive behaviors creeping in
Looking to change way of life with exercise and emotional fitness

No Compulsive Behavior   No Drugs, Alcohol
Aerobic Exercise   Perfect Diet?

⬆   Winning Level   ⬆

Poker But No Sports   No Pot
Walking   Inconsistent Diet

GA Meetings ⬆ Intermediate Level ⬆
Shrink
AA Meetings

Degenerate Gambling   Drugs
No Exercise   Bad Food

Addict Level

Could you imagine where your life would be if you never allowed compulsive or destructive thoughts to enter your mind?

If you are gambling or doing drugs, drinking alcohol, eating bad food and never exercising, you're at the addict level. At the intermediate level, you are going to meetings, you have a shrink, you are talking to some friends, and you are making progress. If you can get yourself above that—no gaming, a lot of exercise (even walking), and no substances—you are working your way up to the winning level.

At that point, compulsive behaviors will start to disappear, aerobic exercise will start to feel good, and being on the perfect diet and not drinking or doing drugs will start to really be exciting.

If you are anything like me, you know what it's like when your day-to-day plan revolves around casinos and card games or drugs and alcohol; far from the winning level. Have you done battle at the poker table or with your pot pipe? *I never met a bud I wouldn't smoke.* Maybe you've hung out with fat slobs and bookies, or sports whizzes who gamble all day and night on their computers, or those dealers who travel with triple-beam scales.

At the winning level, we feel contented. We lose interest in judging other people and develop the ability to enjoy every moment. We start to enjoy the absence of conflict our lives. Most importantly, we lose the ability to worry and begin to experience frequent episodes of smiling and appreciation. We feel tied to others in nature. We let things happen rather than make them happen, and we become more sensitive to the love extended by other people, and feel the urge to extend our love as well.

Put your past behind you. Do not let childhood scripts dictate how you live your life today. Getting better means speaking truth and developing skills that you did not have as a kid. For example, you will need to be able to identify the scripts and understand how they affect your current life. You will also need to know how to prevent script-based behavior.

I have seen my results from the Beck depression test, AKA the hopelessness scale, the anxiety inventory, and the OCD symptoms checklist. I was done looking at the world as a contaminated place that required me to clean, hoard, and constantly check. It was time to let the distress go.

You cannot let shame and guilt rule your recovery. Base your recovery on actions, not reactions. Express your feelings in healthy ways, and learn self-love and self-acceptance. By doing this, you will set healthy new boundaries and limits. You will be able to play, relax, grow, and be intimate.

Key to life

Symptoms
Thinking I can fix it myself
Defiant
Bad habits
Tension
Putting up barriers

"Key To Life!!!"

I Can Do It Myself

"X" Comes in through the back door
("X" Thrives on your isolation)

Defiance

You

If you are being defiant, submission will help you heal. Submission will keep you in the center channel and taking direction from people who can help you. The mere act of following someone else's plan will help you immensely to overcome this defiance. Just submit and work it. Practice this concept.

To deal with tension, you must be able to address it the moment it occurs. This is the real solution. Do not resort to primitive ways of dealing with tension. Instead let an outflow occur, and use this as a tool for releasing the tension. Bringing it on and letting it go is crucial in the healing process.

We live in an impenetrable system of denial. To break that which is ingrained in our souls is the intervention. Sometimes it takes a major force to confront and penetrate the barriers that we put up. The interventionist, who can be a family member or a professional, will dramatically show the damage the addict has caused in the hopes of getting that individual to realize they must take some action.

All the crises and problems we create for ourselves cause us to seek change. We all go through stages that allow us to accept certain plans of recovery. The time for an intervention is as soon as possible. I am sure that some of you reading this book want to do an intervention for someone, and some of you are reading this book need to be intervened.

Preparing for it will let you see what issues need to be dealt with and what the timeline for dealing with them should be. Just remember, any drug that changes a way a person feels is totally abusable, including marijuana or alcohol. The affect on that person is mood altering, hence they call it a "fix;" fixes your mood. By now you know this is not the be-all and end-all, and most likely the problem is either at home or related to some interpersonal issue. Everything feels good until the drug wears off; then, it is just farther down you go. This will create a cycle of addiction capable of destroying everything in its' path.

These lessons should be thought of as tools. I have described real situations and anxiety-causing problems that might make a person use. I also discussed values and spiritual concepts that remind us of our integrity and of our need to learn how to live free of lies, mayhem, and distrust. It forces us to evaluate our moral condition all the time. Honesty, integrity, and morals are keys to success. What is most important for you to understand is that if you or anyone you know has emotional or physical problems, especially addictions, there is help.

This book is the story of my journey. None of this could have been written without the support and wisdom of Doctor Philip Stutz. It is not meant to replace AA, GA, drug rehab, or a therapist, which certainly can help. I wanted to pass along some of the tools I used as I conquered my problems.

We must love ourselves enough to seek help. There are many treatment centers to choose from, and the United States has premier facilities. California particularly has many different programs. *Jon you live with all the cuckoos.* There are also wonderful programs in Arizona, such as Sierra Tucson. Hazelton, in Minnesota, uses spiritually combined and discipline techniques. Al-Anon is also another great place to start. Al-Anon is a nationwide program that allows meetings to be arranged with co-dependants who suffer from similar addictions.

For teens there are places like the Discovery Academy in Utah and Creative Addiction Recovery in Malibu. Treatment for Teen Addictions and Help My Teen Drug Abuse all have services, information, and books for teens.

For eating disorders, there's Rader Programs, a leading provider of treatment for anorexia, bulimia, and compulsive overeating. Ramada Ranch also provides inpatient programs dedicated to women and girls. Milestones, Del Amo Hospital, and Pale Reflections are also great facilities.

Whether you are a professional, a parent, or a loved one searching for answers, such centers can provide the assistance you need. For some people, detox is necessary, and many facilities offer that as well. It is my experience that in order to recover spiritually, you need to clear your system of all chemicals, especially opiates. Detox techniques vary widely, and I sympathize with anyone facing this process. The fear of physical pain often prevents people from going through with detox, so intervention is suggested. Anything to get to the next step is recommended. It is urgent to take action before devastating consequences occur.

The Internet (Google, Yahoo) is a great resource when it comes to finding information on subjects such as substance abuse, eating disorders, treatment centers, detox, and rehab. Treatment centers have varying philosophies and admissions procedures. When researching treatment facilities, pay attention to such things as what types of codependent programs and after-care programs are offered. Finding a program that fits your needs, and the needs of your family, is very important.

Learning to control addiction and to lead a relatively normal life requires the whole family to become involved. In some cases, treatment resolves violence problems in the family. It can also prevent others from developing addictions and can positively affect families, schools, and communities around you, especially when children and/or teenagers are part of the equation.

Plan of Will

Symptoms
No structure
Lacking a daily plan of action
Discipline at night for next day

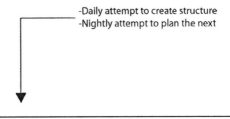

-Daily attempt to create structure
-Nightly attempt to plan the next

Monday ---> Tuesday ---> Wednesday ---> Thursday ---> Friday

"Plane of will"

-Daily Committment
-Daily Action

Stick to your nature. Keep the impulses and the hypercritical negativity out. Try to be constantly disciplined and creative power will follow. That means Monday, Tuesday, Wednesday, Thursday, and Friday all must entail daily attempts to create structure and nightly attempts to plan the next day. That's the key to providing positive steps to success. This leads to a great plan of will with daily commitments and daily actions. That is a model I am committed to need to constantly be reminded of as a key principle of self-expression.

Moment of Decision

Symptoms
Constant bad thoughts during the day
Not choosing the correct direction to go into
Not in touch with the higher path

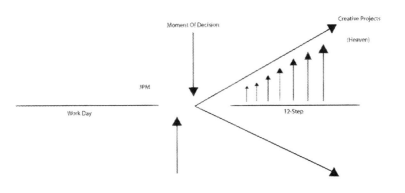

At work, we are constantly confronted with moments of decision. We might find that our day is going fine, but five hours into it we suddenly need excitement, and all of a sudden there is a gap. *You taking the high channel or the low channel this time Jon?*

Avoiding a deformed day is so important. *Make sure you take all of your medicine Jon. If you told yourself you were going to exercise, then do it, lazy. And if you avoid that dinner tonight with your father, I'll laugh at you.* To do that, we need to be disciplined and determined; this will lead to greater satisfaction on a daily basis. We must feel something that is invisible to lead us from deformed structures in our days to wonderful lives. We need to take that straight path during our workday. At that moment of decision, we need to go up into our heaven, not down into our hell.

If addiction is threatening to ruin the life of a loved one, and you do not know what to do, please consider passing this information along to friends and family. It might help you to join together and take some needed action; possibly even conduct an intervention. You might be considering trying a whole host of other well-intended strategies before you attempt an intervention, but most of these efforts have probably already been tried in the past.

Speaking from experience, I know how difficult it is for an addict to truly understand the impact of their behaviors. It is hard for them to break the vicious cycle of denial that they live in. If you need to, work with an interventionist or a paid professional when making decisions about such issues as where and when you will intervene and who will be present at the meeting.

If the intervention will be a surprise, you need to figure out what plans must be made to ensure the person will attend. You will also need to make sure that no one spoils the surprise. Some people may ask to write letters to loved ones during the intervention. The purpose of this process is to get the addict to agree to enter a treatment program.

I hope that you now realize that a higher power is there for everybody. I hope that this book has been a motivator. I hope that any deadlines you were facing before are no longer making you feel anxious. I hope that you are not stressing or having as many sleepless nights. I hope that you are reconsidering seeking counseling or reevaluating your medication. If you do indulge in any kinds of fast escapes, I hope you can finally realize that ultimately those things will leave you empty.

If you are an enabler, I hope that you stop covering up for the person you are enabling. I hope that you are not trying to control the addict and that you are not letting the addict control you.

If you are not an addict, I hope that you have thought about your values and your intentions and how you can restore them, and how you can help the addict restore them. I hope you've seen through some of my experiences what the addict is going through: the person, the situation, the environment, the experience, and all the bad phases of life. You will realize, as I did, that addiction is an inadequate satisfaction.

I ended up failing to get the feeling that I needed. I was just trying to escape from misery, trying to return to some form of ecstasy, and it did not work.

If you or someone you know is involved in binge drinking, self-destructiveness, low self-esteem, or bad health, these things need to be worked on. You can restore your values; you can create solid citizens by turning them in the right direction. Whether you are a hospital worker, a student, a family man, a father, a mother, a husband, a wife, a brother, or a sister, please do not allow addicts to sacrifice their moral values and prostitute their lives into a lower level of thinking.

You could possibly mature out of addiction, but it is doubtful. I would not recommend that approach. Addiction does not go away on its' own. Cutting back on drug use is not the way to quit. You have to realize that you cannot control other people's behaviors.

The only way you can feel good is by using some substance that changes your feelings, and you need to realize that that substance is love.

Some addicts have been diagnosed with mental illness. In many cases, the mental illness might have come before the alcoholism or addiction. Even if you are having obsessive thoughts of death or you are blaming people for other situations, try to remember that a sense of positive energy will motivate you and make you feel better. Do not allow your motivations to get out of hand, and certainly don't think that by constantly changing jobs, traveling, or moving that you are fixing things, because you're not.

Don't feel alone, whoever you are. At least one in ten employees will succumb to an addictive disease at some time in their lives. There are probably people like this where you work. No matter how careful an organization's employment process is, it is impossible to identify every addict. But this is reality, and everyone is affected.

Lastly, I want to say, from a gambling addict's point of view, that what I see in casinos today is glitter and glamour. They are brainwashing everyone through TV. Unfortunately, new addicts are being born as we speak. These poor children do not even realize how ugly their lives will become. The Internet gaming sites and all of the local casinos popping up on Indian reservations are countless.

In just five years there will be many millions of new gamblers at the bottom.

Jon you better clean up or you are going to wind up dead like your friends.

Relaxing is part of my new prescription, along with having new optimism about my future and envisioning new friends and health and a new set of goals and values. I had to focus on letting go of all the traumas from childhood. I have to work on allowing my brain to release the right chemicals as opposed to the old chemicals. This allows me to experience inspiration and to find solutions that will help me gain the right consciousness, one that will let me experience happiness. Gambling was a waste of my power. Structure, discipline and an outflow of love are my salvation. Many have told me that I have something known as synchronicity attraction. This means that I attract whatever I am interested in. By cleaning up my act, I can transmit and receive these messages. It's spontaneous. It allows the new values, ideals, and dreams to become a reality.

I chose life over death. I decided to take responsibility for my actions. Please do not think of this as something trendy like birth charts and solar return ideas. This is simply about energy that pushes up against us and leaves us with better communication. It also keeps us from having our energy stolen and from risking our relationships drifting away. It fights chaos and replaces it with peace and self-empowerment.

Gamblers and addicts are always searching for a higher state and for winning environments. Highs, lows, winning, and losing create unpredictable styles just like drinking and boozing do. What most gamblers do not realize is that there are hip, calm, cool people waiting for them to arrive. Some of these people are disguised as beautiful women, tall and sexy, and some are foreigners that mask their genius. Others are young and smart and have giant IQs and are waiting to take you for all you've got. Gamblers need to realize that these people aren't going to rescue them from emotional distress.

Gamblers need to change their thoughts, find love, and fix their broken hearts. Gambling and addictive behavior won't fill that hole in your soul. These things simply let the devil in the door.

Creating structure in your day will give you power and keep you from all the annoyances and chaos. Balance and unity will help you set limits and deal with resentments. If you have kids, play with them. I found that this is a great "stress buster" and helps provide balance. Imperfection is OK.

My thoughts, words, and deeds create my present as well as my future. It makes it possible to love myself. Uncertainty takes all my energy, and I try to fight it with an inspiration that will allow me to face the world without fear.

I am constantly looking for amazement and opportunities to find reassurance. Anything to avoid sleepwalking through life. For me, all of these little miracles are like corrections.

Miracles pave the way for love and cancel out interference. Miracles let good memories continue. Miracles allow givers to give and receivers to receive. Miracles alter order, heal, and offer forgiveness. They are proof that a higher force is working in all of our lives.

Treatment Centers

AdCare Hospital of Worcester, Inc.—Massachusetts
Addiction Recovery Resources of New Orleans—Louisiana
ADDLife Addiction Services—South Carolina
Advanced Recovery Center—Florida
AEG—Aspen Achievement Academy—Utah
AEG—Aspen Ranch—Utah
AEG—Excel Academy—Texas
AEG—Passages to Recovery—Utah
AEG—SunHawk Academy—Utah
Alcoholic Rehabilitation Association—ARA—Idaho
Alta Vista Recovery Program at Memorial Center—California
Alternative Youth Care—Montana
Alternatives in Treatment—Florida
Amity Circle Tree Ranch—Arizona
Anasazi Foundation—Arizona
Archway Communities Inc.—Missouri
Arizona Pathways—Arizona
Atchison Valley Hope—Kansas
Avia House—California
Avery House/Halfway House for Women & Children—Maryland
Awakenings—Ohio
Bay Recovery Centers, Inc.—California
The Beachcomber Rehabilitation, Inc.—Florida
Beacon House—California
Behavioral Health of the Palm Beaches—Florida
Behavioural Health Foundation, Inc.—Manitoba

Bellin Psychiatric Center—Wisconsin
Bellwood Health Service—Ontario
Betty Ford Center—California
Blue Mountain House of Hope, Inc.—Pennsylvania
Boonville Valley Hope—Missouri
Broadway Lodge—England
Broe Rehabilitation Services, Inc.—Michigan
Brookhaven Hospital—Oklahoma
BryLin Hospitals—New York
Buffalo Valley Inc.—Tennessee
Burning Tree Recovery Ranch—Texas
Calvary Ranch—California
Calvary Rehabilitation Center—Arizona
Calvert County Treatment Facility—Maryland
Canton-Potsdam Hospital—New York
Caron Foundation—Pennsylvania
Casa de Amigas—Arizona
Catherine Freer Wilderness Therapy Expeditions—Oregon
Cedar House Rehabilitation Center—California
Cedar Mountain Treatment Center—Wyoming
Challenges—Florida
Chandler Valley Hope—Arizona
Chapman House, Inc.—California
Charlford House Society for Women—British Columbia
Chester A. Ray Center—Michigan
Chestnut Health Systems—Illinois
Cinnamon Hills Youth Crisis Center—Utah
Colonial House, Inc.—Pennsylvania
Comeback Treatment Center—California
COPAC, Inc.—Mississippi
Cornerstone of Medical Arts Hospital—New York
Cornerstone of Rhinebeck—New York

Cornerstone of Southern California—California
Cottonwood de Tucson—Arizona
Crossroads Antigua—Antigua, West Indies
Crossroads Centre Inc.—Ontario
Crossroads for Women—Maine
Cumberland Heights—Tennessee
Cushing Valley Hope—Oklahoma
Deep Run Lodge—Virginia
Desert Canyon Treatment Center—Arizona
The Discovery Program—California
DOT Caring Centers, Inc.—Michigan
Drug Abuse Research (DARE) Bahay Pagasa Therapeutic
    Community—Philippines
Eagleville Hospital—Pennsylvania
Edgewood Chemical Dependency Treatment Centre—British
    Columbia
Endeavor House—New Jersey
Fairfax Hospital—Washington
Fairwinds Treatment Center—Florida
Father Martin's Ashley—Maryland
Fellowship Club St. Paul—Minnesota
Florida Center for Recovery Inc.—Florida
Focus Healthcare at High Point—Florida
Focus Healthcare at MeadowWood Hospital—Delaware
Focus Healthcare of Ohio—Ohio
Gateway Recovery Systems—Louisiana
Gateway Rehabilitation Center—Pennsylvania
Giordano & Goldfarb's Holistic Treatment Program—Florida
Gosnold on Cape Cod—Massachusetts
Grapevine Valley Hope—Texas
Green Villa—Texas
Gray Wolf Ranch—Washington

Guest House—Men—Minnesota
Guest House—Women—Michigan
Habilitat, Inc.—Hawaii
Hanley-Hazelden—Florida
Harbor Oaks Hospital—Michigan
Harmony Foundation—Colorado
Harrison House of Virginia—Virginia
Hazelden—Minnesota
Hazelden Center for Youth & Families—Minnesota
Hazelden Springbrook—Oregon
Highland Hospital—West Virginia
Hope Valley, Inc.—North Carolina
Hyde Park Counseling Center—Florida
Illinois Institute for Addiction Recovery—Illinois
International Rehabilitation Centers, Inc.—Jamaica
International Rehabilitation Centers, Inc.—Mexico
Island Grove Regional Treatment Center—Colorado
Jellema House—Pathfinder Resources—Michigan
Jellinek Clinic—The Netherlands
The Journey Home—Louisiana
Kent House, Inc.—Rhode Island
Keystone Treatment Center—South Dakota
KidsPeace National Centers for Kids in Crisis—Pennsylvania
Kingsboro Alcoholism Treatment Center—New York
La Hacienda Treatment Center—Texas
Lakeside-Milam Recovery Centers—Washington
Last Door Recovery Centre—British Columbia
Laurelwood Center—Mississippi
La Verna Lodge—Indiana
Liberty House—California
Life Center Foundation Inc.—Tennessee
Life Center of Galax—Virginia

Life's Journey Center—California
Lifeskills of Boca Raton—Florida
Lisa Merlin House, Inc.—Florida
Little Hill—Alina Lodge—New Jersey
Lloyd Noland Hospital—Alabama
Mainstream K.C., Inc.—Kansas
Malvern Institute—Pennsylvania
Manhattan Addiction Treatment Center—New York
Manning Family Recovery Center—Iowa
Maple Leaf Farm Association, Inc.—Vermont
Marworth Treatment Center—Pennsylvania
Meadows, The—Arizona
Memorial Hermann Prevention & Recovery Center
    (PaRC)—Texas
Memphis Recovery Centers, Inc.—Tennessee
Meriter Hospital—New Start Program—Wisconsin
Metro Atlanta Recovery Residences, Inc.—Georgia
Metropolitan Serenity House, Inc.—Georgia
Michael's House—The Treatment Center for Men—California
Minnesota Teen Challenge—Minnesota
Mountainside Treatment Center—Connecticut
MPI Chemical Dependency Treatment Services—California
Mrs. Wilson's Halfway House—New Jersey
Narconon Arrowhead—Oklahoma
Narconon Newport Beach—California
Nelson L. Price Treatment Center, The—Georgia
New Beginnings at Waverly—Minnesota
New Beginnings Home Program—Florida
New Directions for Women, Inc.—California
New Found Life, Inc.—California
New Hope Manor—New York
New Life Treatment Center—Minnesota

Newark Beth Israel Medical Center—New Jersey
Northwestern Institute of Psychiatry—Pennsylvania
Norton Valley Hope—Kansas
Oasis Treatment Center—California
O'Brien House—Louisiana
Olalla Recovery Centers—Washington
Older Adult Recovery Services: Wake Forest University Baptist
     Medical Center—North Carolina
O'neill Valley Hope—Nebraska
Orchard Recovery Center Ltd.—British Columbia
Pacific Hills Treatment Center—California
Palm Beach Institute, The—Florida
Palmetto Addiction Recovery Center—Louisiana
Parker Valley Hope—Colorado
Pathway Family Center—Michigan
Pathways Treatment Center—Montana
The Pavilion—Illinois
Pavillon International—North Carolina
Penn Foundation Recovery Center—Pennsylvania
Philip House—New Jersey
Pia's Place, Inc.—Arizona
Power House I—Louisiana
Power House II—Louisiana
Prescott House—Arizona
Progress Valley I—Men's Residence—Minnesota
Progress Valley II—Women's Residence—Minnesota
Progress Valley Phoenix—Coed Residence—Arizona
Promises Treatment Centers—California
Ranch, The—Tennessee
Recovery Acres Society—Alberta
Recovery Centers of Arkansas—Arkansas
Recovery Resources, Inc.—Illinois

Red Rock Canyon School—Utah
Renaissance Institute of Palm Beach—Florida
Renaissance Project, Inc.—New York
Renewal Center—Pennsylvania
Ridgeview Institute—Georgia
Rimrock Foundation—Montana
River Oaks Hospital—Louisiana
RiverValley Behavioral Health—Kentucky
St. Joseph's Rehabilitation Center, Inc.—New York
St. Jude Retreat House—New York
St. Jude's Residence—New Hampshire
St. Lawrence Addiction Treatment Center—New York
Saint Vincent's Hospital—New York
Samhjalp Foundation—Iceland
Santulan—India
Savannas Hospital—Florida
Schick Shadel Hospital—Washington
Seabrook House—New Jersey
Seacliff Recovery Center—California
Self Help Addiction Rehabilitation (SHAR), Inc.—Michigan
Serenity House—Virginia
Serenity Lane—Oregon
ShareHouse—North Dakota
Sierra Recovery Center—California
Sierra Tucson—Arizona
Silver Hill—Connecticut
Simon House Recovery Centre—Alberta
Sleepy Valley Center—New York
Sober Living By The Sea—California
South Miami Hospital Addiction Treatment Program—Florida
So Tier Addiction Rehabilitation Services—New York
Spruce Mountain Inn—Vermont

SSTAR, Inc.—Massachusetts
Starlite Recovery Center—Texas
Stepping Stones Addiction Centre—South Africa
Stonington Institute—Connecticut
Stutzman Alcoholism Treatment Center—New York
Summer House—Florida
Sundown M Ranch—Washington
Sunrise House Foundation, Inc.—New Jersey
Substance Abuse Foundation of Long Beach—California
Synergy Treatment Centers—Tennessee
Talbott Recovery Campus—Georgia
Tara Treatment Center—Indiana
10 Acre Ranch—California
Transitions Recovery Program—Florida
Trinity Recovery Center, Homeward Bound Inc.—Texas
TRS Behavioral Care, Inc.—The Next Step—Texas
TRS Behavioral Care, Inc.—The Right Step—Texas
Tully Hill Alcohol & Drug Treatment Center—New York
Turning Point Hospital—Georgia
Turning Point of Tampa—Florida
Turquoise Lodge—New Mexico
Twelve Oaks—Florida
Two Rivers Psychiatric Hospital—Missouri
Valley Hope at Halstead Hospital—Kansas
Valley Forge Medical Center & Hospital—Pennsylvania
Van Dyke Addiction Treatment Center—New York
Villa San José—Costa Rica
Warwick Manor Behavioral Health, Inc.—Maryland
Waryas House—New York
White Buffalo Youth Inhalant Treatment Centre—Saskatchewan
White Deer Run—Pennsylvania
Wilderness Quest/Blue Mountain Family Center—Utah

Wilderness Treatment Center—Montana
William J. McCord Adolescent Treatment Facility—South
    Carolina
Willingway Hospital—Georgia
Williamsburg Place & The William J. Farley Center—Virginia
Willough at Naples, The—Florida
Wilp Si Satxw—British Columbia
Women's Odyssey Organization, Inc.—California
Women's Recovery Association (WRA)—California
Wyoming Substance Abuse Treatment & Recovery Center

ALABAMA	Lloyd Noland Hospital
ARIZONA	Amity Circle Tree Ranch
	Anasazi Foundation
	Calvary Rehabilitation Center
	Casa de Amigas
	Desert Canyon Treatment Center
	Pia's Place, Inc.
	Progress Valley Phoenix—Coed Residence
	Sierra Tucson
ARKANSAS	Recovery Centers of Arkansas
CALIFORNIA	Betty Ford Center
	Calvary Ranch
	Cedar House Rehabilitation Center
	Comeback Treatment Center
	The Discovery Program
	Michael's House—The Treatment Center for Men
	MPI Chemical Dependency Treatment Services
	New Directions for Women, Inc.
	Pacific Hills Treatment Center
	Promises Treatment Centers
	Seacliff Recovery Center
	10-Acre Ranch—California
	Women's Recovery Association (WRA)
COLORADO	Island Grove Regional Treatment Center
	Harmony Foundation
	Parker Valley Hope
CONNECTICUT	Mountainside Treatment Center
	Silver Hill
	Stonington Institute
DELAWARE	Focus Healthcare at Meadow Wood Hospital

FLORIDA	Alternatives in Treatment The Beachcomber Rehabilitation, Inc Giordano & Goldfarb's Holistic Treatment Program Lifeskills of Boca Raton Lisa Merlin House, Inc Challenges Focus Healthcare at High Point Hanley-Hazelden South Miami Hospital Addiction Treatment Program Transitions Recovery Program Willough at Naples, The
GEORGIA	Metro Atlanta Recovery Residences, Inc Metropolitan Serenity House, Inc Nelson L. Price Treatment Center, The Turning Point Hospital Willingway Hospital
HAWAII	Habilitat, Inc
IDAHO	Alcoholic Rehabilitation Association—ARA
ILLINOIS	Chestnut Health Systems Illinois Institute for Addiction Recovery Recovery Resources, Inc
INDIANA	La Verna Lodge Tara Treatment Center
IOWA	Manning Family Recovery Center
KANSAS	Atchison Valley Hope Mainstream K.C., Inc Norton Valley Hope
KENTUCKY	RiverValley Behavioral Health

LOUISIANA	Addiction Recovery Resources of New Orleans
	Gateway Recovery Systems
	The Journey Home
	O'Brien House
	Palmetto Addiction Recovery Center
	River Oaks Hospital
MAINE	Crossroads for Women
MARYLAND	Avery House/Halfway House for Women & Children
	Warwick Manor Behavioral Health, Inc.
MASSACHUSETTS	AdCare Hospital of Worcester, Inc.
	Gosnold on Cape Cod
MICHIGAN	Broe Rehabilitation Services, Inc.
	Chester A. Ray Center
	DOT Caring Centers, Inc
	Harbor Oaks Hospital
	Pathway Family Center
	Self Help Addiction Rehabilitation (SHAR), Inc.
MINNESOTA	Fellowship Club St. Paul
	Hazelden Center for Youth & Families
	Minnesota Teen Challenge
	New Life Treatment Center
	Progress Valley I—Men's Residence
	Progress Valley II—Women's Residence
MISSISSIPPI	COPAC, Inc.
	Laurelwood Center
MISSOURI	Archway Communities Inc.
	Boonville Valley Hope
	Two Rivers Psychiatric Hospital
MONTANA	Alternative Youth Care
	Pathways Treatment Center
	Rimrock Foundation
	Wilderness Treatment Center

NEBRASKA	O'neill Valley Hope
NEW HAMPSHIRE	St. Jude's Residence
NEW JERSEY	Endeavor House Little Hill—Alina Lodge Mrs. Wilson's Halfway House Newark Beth Israel Medical Center Philip House Seabrook House
NEW MEXICO	Turquoise Lodge
NEW YORK	BryLin Hospitals Manhattan Addiction Treatment Center Cornerstone of Medical Arts Hospital New Hope Manor St. Jude Retreat House St. Lawrence Addiction Treatment Center Sleepy Valley Center Stutzman Alcoholism Treatment Center Tully Hill Alcohol & Drug Treatment Center Waryas House
NORTH CAROLINA	Hope Valley, Inc. Older Adult Recovery Services: Wake Forest
NORTH DAKOTA	ShareHouse
OHIO	Awakenings Focus Healthcare of Ohio
OKLAHOMA	Brookhaven Hospital Cushing Valley Hope Narconon Arrowhead
OREGON	Catherine Freer Wilderness Therapy Expeditions Hazelden Springbrook Serenity Lane

PENNSYLVANIA	Blue Mountain House of Hope, Inc
	KidsPeace National Centers for Kids in Crisis
	Colonial House, Inc.
	Gateway Rehabilitation Center
	Malvern Institute
	Northwestern Institute of Psychiatry
	Renewal Center
	White Deer Run
RHODE ISLAND	Kent House, Inc.
SOUTH CAROLINA	ADDLife Addiction Services
	William J. McCord Adolescent Treatment Facility
SOUTH DAKOTA	Keystone Treatment Center
TENNESSEE	Buffalo Valley Inc.
	Cumberland Heights
	Memphis Recovery Centers, Inc.
	Synergy Treatment Centers
TEXAS	Burning Tree Recovery Ranch
	Grapevine Valley Hope
	Green Villa
	Memorial Hermann Prevention & Recovery Center
	Starlite Recovery Center
	Trinity Recovery Center, Homeward Bound Inc
UTAH	Sun Hawk Academy
	Cinnamon Hills Youth Crisis Center
	Wilderness Quest/Blue Mountain Family Center
VERMONT	Maple Leaf Farm Association, Inc.
	Spruce Mountain Inn
VIRGINIA	Deep Run Lodge
	Harrison House of Virginia
	Williamsburg Place & The William J. Farley Center

WASHINGTON	Gray Wolf Ranch
	Olalla Recovery Centers
	Sundown M Ranch
WEST VIRGINIA	Highland Hospital
WISCONSIN	Bellin Psychiatric Center
	Meriter Hospital—New Start Program
WYOMING	Cedar Mountain Treatment Center
	Wyoming Substance Abuse Treatment & Recovery Center
OUTSIDE THE US	Behavioural Health Foundation, Inc.—Manitoba
	Bellwood Health Service—Ontario
	Broadway Lodge—England
	Charlford House Society for Women—British Columbia
	Crossroads Antigua—Antigua, West Indies
	International Rehabilitation Centers, Inc.—Jamaica
	International Rehabilitation Centers, Inc.—Mexico
	Jellinek Clinic—The Netherlands
	Last Door Recovery Centre—British Columbia
	Recovery Acres Society—Alberta
	Samhjalp Foundation—Iceland
	Santulan—India
	Simon House Recovery Centre—Alberta
	Stepping Stones Addiction Centre—South Africa
	Villa San José—Costa Rica
	White Buffalo Youth Inhalant Treatment Centre—Saskatchewan

978-0-595-35864-9
0-595-35864-0

CPSIA information can be obtained at www.ICGtesting.com
Printed in the USA
LVOW11s2015060914

402826LV00001B/23/A